A COLLECTION O

RUDE LIMERICKS

"There once was a naughty boy from Nantucket..."

BEE THREE BOOKS

books by
BOXER
www.booksbyboxer.com

Bee Three Publishing is an imprint of Books By Boxer
Published by
Books By Boxer, Leeds, LS13 4BS UK
Books by Boxer (EU), Dublin D02 P593 IRELAND
© Books By Boxer 2023
All Rights Reserved
MADE IN CHINA
ISBN: 9781915410160

MIX
Paper | Supporting
responsible forestry
FSC™ C007683

This book is produced from responsibly sourced paper to ensure forest management

A short, young psychic called Marge,
Went to Jail on a bad charge.
But when she broke out,
The news was about
A "Small Medium at Large"!

There once was a dental hygienist,
Who sat on an elephant's penis.
The penis errupted,
His backside corrupted,
And now there's a dentist on Venus!

There's a family in Alabama,
Who's auntie is also their mama,
She married her brother,
He went with another,
Now his cousin's baby's their grandma!

There was a young woman named Kitty,
Who won prizes for her big titty,
From the womb she was blessed,
With a cosmic sized breast,
But the other was itty-bitty!

There was a man with little wit,
who couldn't find his girlfriend's clit.
He went on a quest,
From her toes to chest,
Finally settling for her pit!

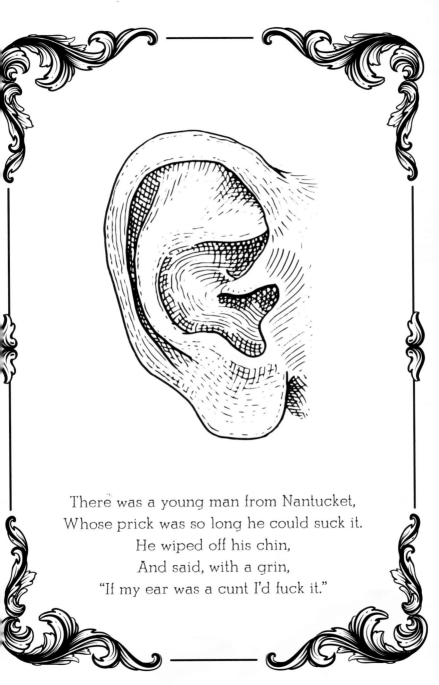

There was a young man from Nantucket,
Whose prick was so long he could suck it.
He wiped off his chin,
And said, with a grin,
"If my ear was a cunt I'd fuck it."

There was a lady from Dubai,
Whose pubes were as rough as cactai.
When she sits on dick,
Men squeal from the prick,
Because thorns stab into their thigh!

There once was an old man called Jim,
Who changed his sex on a whim,
He chopped off his cock,
Stuffed bras with a sock,
And gets triggered by he, she, and him!

There's a Welsh farmer called Jagger,
Who earned the nickname 'sheep-shagger'.
His horse felt inclined,
To mount from behind,
Now Jagger can't help but stagger.

There was an old woman named Mary,
Whose armpits were awfully hairy.
She plaited all the lot,
Tied a bow with a knot,
Now her underarm's not as scary!

Tim had once cheated on his wife,
And hadn't since been seen alive.
His wife made a pie,
With toes and an eye,
I wonder if Tim did survive?

Jade worked hard to go from rags to frocks,
By selling some of her sweaty socks.
A dollar a lick,
A dime for a pic,
Her foot business now has shares in stocks!

Kyle was a rocking hardcore punk,
Who had unbearably cheesy junk,
He was scared of the soap,
His mom had lost all hope,
'Cause he lived in trash like a skunk!

A hungry man went for a Thai,
Complained his meat was very dry,
He went not for a meal,
Just to cop a good feel,
Though he found the Thai was a guy!

Did you hear of the breaking news?
The priest was found upon the pews.
His pants round his ankles,
His willy did dangle,
As he played with the nun's nephews!

A little old man called Roger,
Was a known perverted codger,
He once hired some girls,
who wore fur and pearls,
And played with his wrinkly todger!

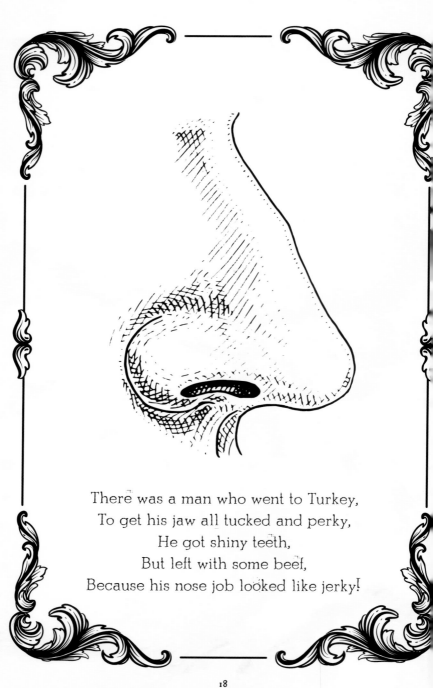

There was a man who went to Turkey,
To get his jaw all tucked and perky,
He got shiny teeth,
But left with some beef,
Because his nose job looked like jerky!

Little Johnny got deported,
Because his backside was distorted.
The tip of his crack,
Reached up Johnny's back,
And his asscheeks weren't supported!

A tragedy befell poor Dave,
Some peace from his wife he did crave.
He bumped his head,
And now he's dead,
But she sits and nags at his grave!

The local witch has a nifty trick,
While riding through night on her broomstick.
Whilst navigating with maps,
She holds the broom with her flaps,
And makes onlookers feel a bit sick!

Down the road is the local bum,
Who sells bottles of his cold cum.
It's like sweet mayonnaise,
Or a thick doughnut glaze,
You shouldn't yuck another's yum!

When it comes to touching a chode,
There's no enigma to decode.
Just a tug and a lick,
It's like lighting a wick,
And watching a fat bomb explode!

Old-fashioned Sue is a bit of a prude,
But behind closed doors she gets a bit rude.
With her legs to the ceiling,
She really likes the feeling,
Of being railed by more than one dude!

There once was a man from Bel Air,
Who did do his wife on the stair.
But the banister broke,
So he doubled his stroke,
And finished her off in mid-air!

There was a young maid from Madras,
Who had a magnificent ass.
Not rounded and pink,
As you might just think,
But grey, had long ears, and ate grass!

There was a young sailor named Bates,
Who danced the fandango on skates.
But a fall on his cutlass,
Has just rendered him nutless,
And practically useless on dates.

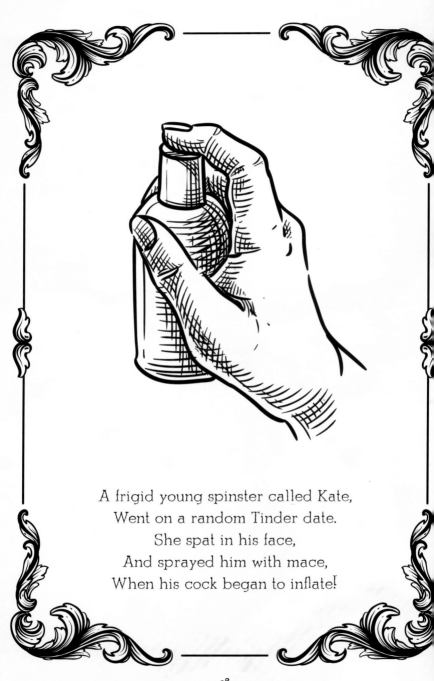

A frigid young spinster called Kate,
Went on a random Tinder date.
She spat in his face,
And sprayed him with mace,
When his cock began to inflate!

A Mafia boss called Big Tony,
was found out to be a big phony.
His big drug cartel,
It had a dry spell,
So he sold bags of crushed macaroni!

There was a young man called Brett,
Who liked to get high on ket.
He soon felt remorse,
When he became a horse,
And was castrated by a vet!

A local girl was charged with murder,
But nobody knew what had spurred her.
They found an old sock,
round a chopped off cock,
And a severed hand on her girder!

There was an old sailor called Marge,
Whose backside was really quite large.
She tucked and she squeezed,
'Til her asshole sneezed,
Blowing holes in the side of the barge!

A spotty old hooker named sally,
Had a vag as wide as a valley.
She could take a man's fist,
All the way to his wrist,
As she did business in the alley!

There was an old man named Bob,
Who was a bit of a slob.
He had stains down his shirt,
From his custard dessert,
And ketchup all round his gob!

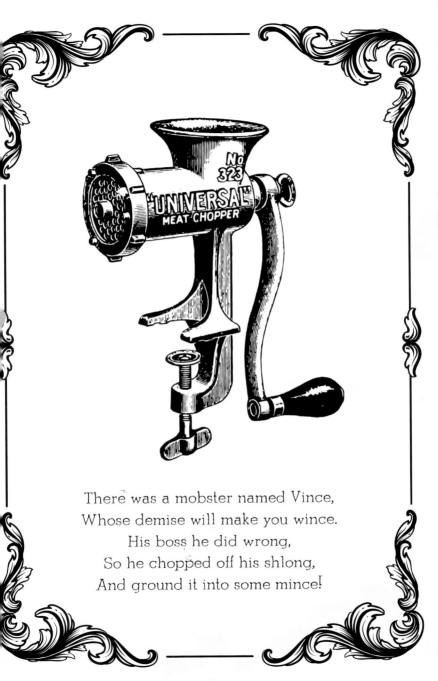

There was a mobster named Vince,
Whose demise will make you wince.
His boss he did wrong,
So he chopped off his shlong,
And ground it into some mince!

Bethany once had a boyfriend,
Who's asshole she needed to tend,
He was found begging,
For a good pegging,
'Til she ripped his hairy backend!

There was a man who would fart,
And claim it a work of art.
To be really frank,
His underwear stank,
When he blew his cheeks apart!

There once was a man named Seamus,
Who became globally famous.
He slept with a whale,
Grew fins and turned pale,
And a tail popped from his anus!

There was a woman from Haiti,
Whose newborn was rather weighty.
It had stretched her vagina,
Birthing the minor,
Now her flaps make her look eighty!

There was a man from Tokyo,
Who was nicknamed Pinocchio.
"It's not what you think"
He said with a wink,
"Telling lies will make my cock grow!"

There once was a butcher named Lee,
Who was as stupid as can be.
He spent all his coins,
On juicy steak loins,
When he could have got them for free.

Alice in Wonderland found a maze,
She was stuck there for weeks and for days.
Turns out she was tripping,
Shroom tea she'd been sipping,
From porcelain cups on silverware trays!

There's a man who was wrong in the head,
He skinned his victims once they were dead.
He made a posh hat,
From his girlfriend's fat,
And a lampshade from faces and thread!

There once was a tall man named Jock,
Who had an extremely long cock,
He wrapped it around,
His tummy and down,
Through his shorts and into his sock.

There once was a man from Gosham,
Who took out his balls to wash 'em.
His wife said "Jack!,
You put 'em back,
Or I'll grab your balls and squash 'em!".

There once was an old man called Dave,
Who dug up a prostitutes grave.
She smelled quite a bit,
And was missing a tit,
But look at the money he saved!

There was a young man from Bombay,
Who screwed 20 chickens a day,
He wouldn't stop fucking,
'Til they started clucking,
Then he'd eat the eggs that they lay.

There once was an old man from Harrow,
Who tried to have sex with a sparrow,
The sparrow said "No,
You can't have a go,
As my asshole is far too narrow".

A fish and a frog went to tea,
With a cat, a dog, and a bee.
The bee lost a wing,
and the tip of his sting,
So the fish and the frog ate for free!

There was a young man named Alfred,
Whose penis was made out of lead.
A girl turned bright green,
Like on Halloween,
When she gave his willy some head!

At my local McDonald's in Surrey,
I spilt tea on my crotch in a scurry,
I had to act quick,
To cool down my dick,
So I stuck it in my cold McFlurry!

On the breast of a barmaid named Gail,
Was tattooed the price of all her ale.
And on her behind,
Because of the blind,
Was the same information in braille!

There once was a man from St. Lou,
Who gave his dear sister a screw.
He said with aplomb:,
"You're better than Mom." ,
Said she: "That's what Dad told me too."

Two lesbians north of the town,
Made sixty–nine love on the ground.
Their unbridled lust,
Leaked out in the dust,
And made so much mud that they drowned.

There once was a fellow O'Doole,
Who found some red spots on his tool.
His Doctor a cynic,
Said get out my clinic,
And wipe off that lipstick you fool!

There once was a guy named Swartz,
Whose dick was covered with warts.
But the girls would still play,
With his dick anyway,
'Cause good ol' Swartz came in quarts!

In the Garden of Eden sat Adam,
Complacently stroking his madam.
And he thought with mirth,
On the whole damned Earth,
There were only two balls and he had 'em.

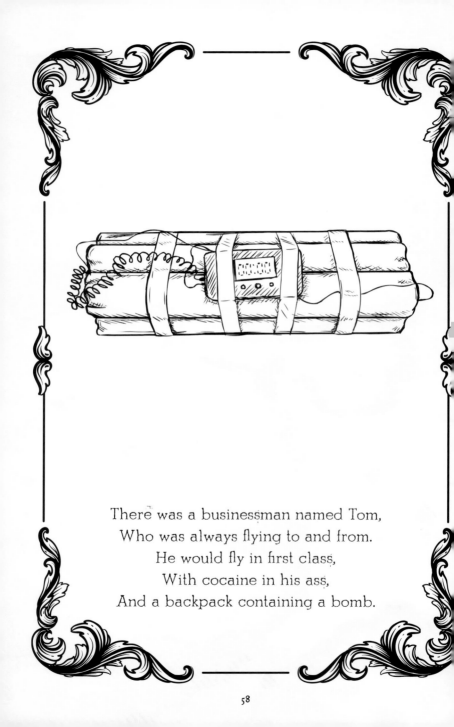

There was a businessman named Tom,
Who was always flying to and from.
He would fly in first class,
With cocaine in his ass,
And a backpack containing a bomb.

There was a woman named Julie,
Who acted rather unruly.
The trip to her villa,
Was more than vanilla,
'Cause she whipped her husband cruelly!

There was a cyclist named Reuben,
Who cycled while smoking a cuban.
He dropped his cigar,
Crashed into a car,
Now his mouth and nose have tubes in.

There is a designer called Mandy,
Whose job can be pretty handy.
She prints counterfeit cash,
And hides it in a stash,
Then spends it on bottles of Brandy!

There was a young girl called Rachel,
Who was a little unstable.
Instead of a pistol,
She uses her crystal,
To wish an accident fatal!

There was an assassin named Olga,
Her resume read rather vulgar.
She thought that the thrill,
Was reason to kill,
But assassins get paid – no one told her!

There was a hydrated man named Chris,
Who just couldn't hold in his piss.
He aimed for the bottle,
His stream went full throttle,
And he soiled his pants from the miss.

There was an accountant named Mo,
Who would launder other folk's dough.
He's wanted abroad,
For sums of tax fraud,
But now where did Mo's money all go?

There's an adventurous girl named Mahri,
Who went on an African safari.
She raced a wild cheetah
That just couldn't beat her,
Because she was driving a Ferrari!

There was a fisherman named Jake,
Whose poor liver really did ache,
He drank so much beer,
It came out of his rear,
And killed all the fish in the lake!

There was a banker named Benjamin,
Who could be a lot more genuine,
You can plead down the phone
He won't give you a loan,
Considering how much debt you're in!

There once was a woman named Trina,
Who dreamed she would be hyena.
One night she awoke,
The window she broke,
And since then, not a soul has seen her!

There was an older inmate named Kevin,
Been in prison since he was eleven.
Stole a six pack of beers,
He got twenty-five years,
His lawyer said he'd only serve seven!

There once was a woman called Ellie,
Who fell asleep watching the telly.
The fridge door she'd left open,
When she woke she was hopin',
That her milk hadn't turned to jelly.

A beautiful, young maiden named Millie,
Was partial to a bit of old willy,
Since it was so mature,
It was cold to the core,
And shriveled from being a bit chilly!

There was a young biker named Keely,
Who engaged in some touchy-feely,
She slipped in a digit,
Then started to fidget,
And when she came she did a wheelie!

There was a man named Steve,
Whose farts could make you heave.
The stench was so bad,
It killed off a lad,
and his colleagues still can't breathe!

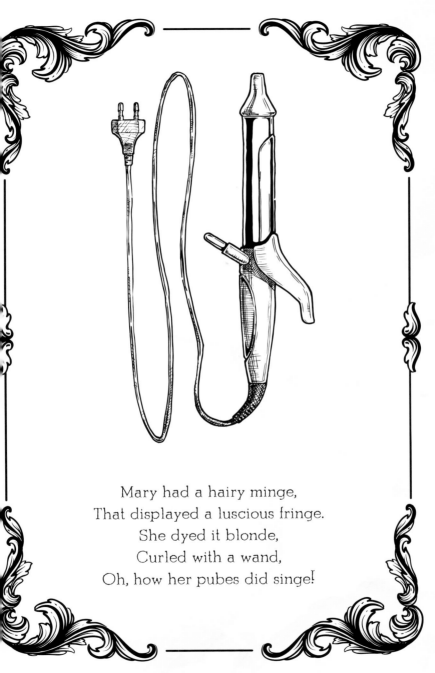

Mary had a hairy minge,
That displayed a luscious fringe.
She dyed it blonde,
Curled with a wand,
Oh, how her pubes did singe!

There was a felon named Frank,
Who held at gunpoint a bank.
The piles of money,
Were wet and runny,
'Cause excitement made him wank!

There was a handsome, tanned Greek,
Who perfected his technique.
He picked and he flicked,
He stroked and he licked...
To clear mucus from his beak!

A friend of mine went to Amsterdam,
And was caught in an unruly scam.
He paid for red lights,
And girls in net tights,
But instead got a joint of roast ham!

A forgetful gasman named Dieter,
Went interfering with his gas heater.
Hit a leak with his lighter,
Then his eyebrows burned brighter,
And his nose hairs became somewhat neater!

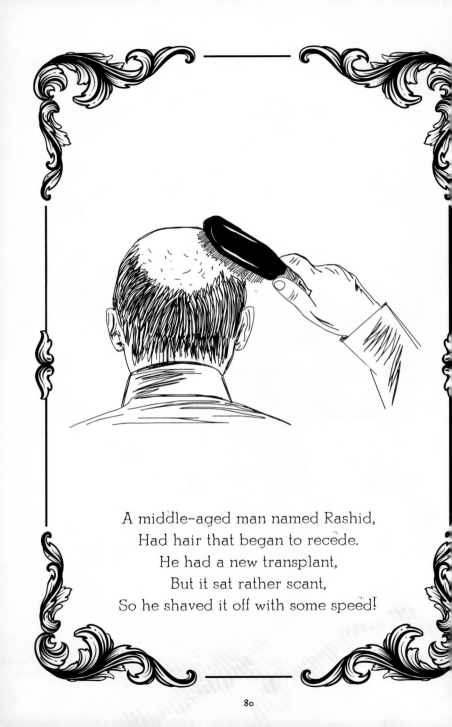

A middle-aged man named Rashid,
Had hair that began to recede.
He had a new transplant,
But it sat rather scant,
So he shaved it off with some speed!

An inanimate sex doll named Candy,
Made her owner a little too randy.
They travelled to a beach,
And he let out a screech,
'Cause her insides were a little too sandy!

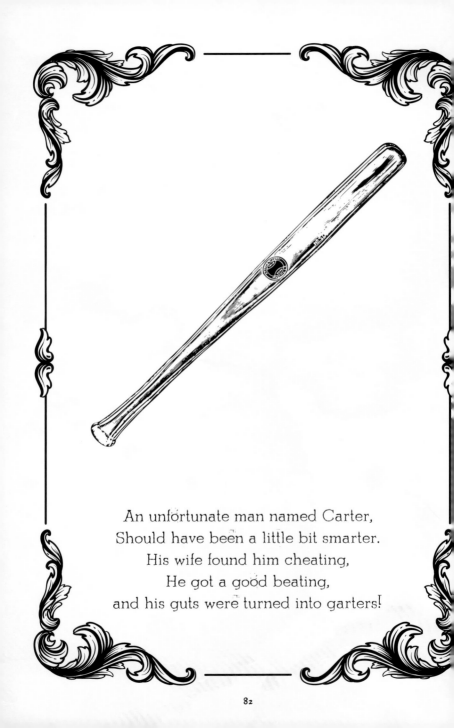

An unfortunate man named Carter,
Should have been a little bit smarter.
His wife found him cheating,
He got a good beating,
and his guts were turned into garters!

There once was a man from Rangoon,
Whose farts could be heard on the moon.
When you'd least expect 'em,
They'd burst from his rectum,
With the force of a raging typhoon.

There was a young woman called Mabel,
Who seemed to be somewhat unstable.
Her poor partner Adam,
Really couldn't fathom,
Why she'd given her dog a facial!

Said an ovum one night to a sperm,
"You're a very attractive young germ.
Come and join me, my sweet,
Let our nuclei meet
And in nine months we'll both come to term."

There was once an old pervert called Lyle,
Who found a young lady to defile.
    She needed no coercion,
    So he made his insertion,
And he polished her off doggy style.

There was a ladyboy from Nantucket,
Who intended to pee in a bucket;
But being a man,
She missed the damn can,
And so away she fled, crying: "Fuck it!"

Down the shaft of Jack's hard flue,
Little Jill had blew and blew.
It was not the air,
Left Jill in despair,
But her nostril full of goo!

On the sandy coast of Guinea,
Was a poor old man named Jimmy.
To afford some bread,
His legs he had spread,
And his ball sack he did shimmy!

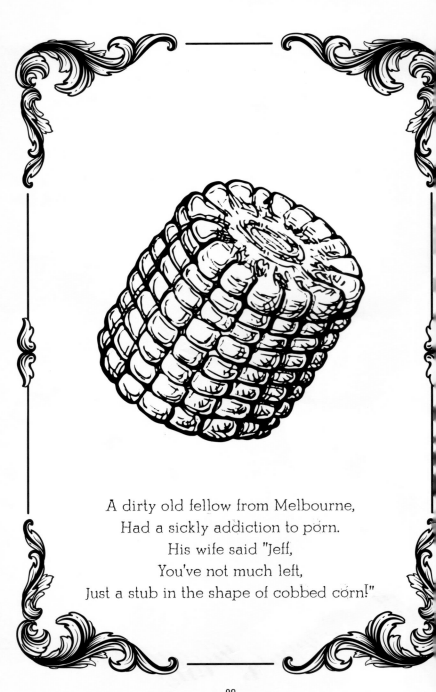

A dirty old fellow from Melbourne,
Had a sickly addiction to porn.
His wife said "Jeff,
You've not much left,
Just a stub in the shape of cobbed corn!"

There once was a man from Topeka,
Who sprinkled his dick with paprika.
The next girl he plowed,
Was screaming so loud,
They heard her in old Tanganyika!

There was a young lady named Ann Titchin,
Who was scratching her crotch in the kitchen,
Her mother said "Rose,
It's crabs I suppose.",
She said "Yes and the fuckers are itchin'!"

That girl from Taiwan was a prize,
With those big, beautiful brown eyes.
Her breasts were well kept,
Just like you'd expect,
But her penis was quite a surprise!

There once was a fellow McSweeny,
Who spilled some gin on his weenie.
Just to be couth,
He added Vermouth,
And slipped his girl a martini!

There was an old whore pulling tricks,
Who at one time handled five pricks,
One day she made a sigh,
As she took out her eye,
And exclaimed "Today, I'll take six!"

There once was a man from Brighton,
Who said "Miss, you're sure a tight one".
She said "I'll burst your bubble,
though it isn't any trouble,
You ain't put your cock in the right one!"

There was a young grocer named Phillipe,
Who sold her body fluids for cheap.
Her insides had grown yeast,
Which she sold as a feast,
And scooped it into bowls in a heap!

There once was a medieval bard,
Who couldn't get his pig's willy hard.
He said with a grin,
"I've got just the thing!",
And smothered its penis with lard!

A blind old lady named Gail,
Had trouble reading with braille,
She fingered the nipple,
Of a surprised cripple,
Then said "What an interesting tale!"

There once was a harlot from Kew,
Who filled her vagina with glue.
She said with a grin,
"If they pay to get in,
They'll pay to get out of it, too!"

There once was a man from Iraq,
Who'd holes down the length of his cock.
When he had an erection,
He could play a collection,
From Johann Sebastian Bach!

A blind old codger called Rick,
Is lethal with his white stick.
Men blocking his path,
Fills him up with wrath,
So he whacks 'em in the dick!

There was a young virgin named Alice,
Who thought of her cunt as a chalice.
One night, sleeping nude,
She woke feeling lewd,
And found in her chalice a phallus!

There was an old man of Australia,
Who felt at a loss (and a failure),
Due to the texture,
And limp architecture,
Of his formerly fine genitalia.

Said the nun as the bishop withdrew,
"Dear, this must be our final adieu,
For the vicar's thicker,
And slicker and quicker,
And five inches longer than you."

There once was a virile young Viking,
Whose sexual prowess was striking.
He would plunder asses,
Of hot Viking lasses,
Each time he found one to his liking.

A lady from South Carolina,
Put fiddle strings 'cross her vagina.
With the proper sized cocks,
What was sex became Bach's
Toccata and Fugue in D Minor.

A newlywed couple named O'Kelly,
Spent their honeymoon belly to belly.
Because in their haste,
They'd used sticky paste,
Instead of petroleum jelly.

There once was a man named Ollie,
Who'd taken far too much molly.
To feel less exposed,
He ripped off his clothes,
And thought his dick was a lolly!

There once was a vampire named Mable,
Who's period was quite unstable.
The night of a full moon,
With the help of a spoon,
She drank herself under the table.

There was an old cougar named June,
Who'd been eaten out with a spoon,
Her insides were ancient,
Had long since being vacant,
And her walls were covered in runes!

An horny pilgrim was on the hunt,
For the tightest and rarest cunt.
With beautiful folds,
And shimmering golds,
Though his sword was mighty blunt!

A dirty old pervert named Rolf,
Had a round of 18 hole golf,
He pulled out his balls,
And all but one falls,
Leaving him the same as Adolf!

From deep in the crypt at St Giles,
Came screaming that carried for miles,
The curate said "Gracious!
Has Father Ignatius,
Forgotten the Bishop's got piles?"

There was a young man from Berlin,
Whose tool was the size of a pin.
Said his girl with a laugh,
As she fondled his shaft,
"Well, this won't be much of a sin."

There once was a plumber from Lee,
Who was plumbing his girl by the sea.
She said "Stop your plumbing,
There's somebody coming!"
Said the plumber still plumbing... "It's me!"

A gay hit a trucker in Laporte,
The vehicle did slightly distort.
Said the irate old trucker,
"Suck my cock, you dumb fucker!",
And they settled the case out of court!

There was a gay Countess of Bray,
You may think it odd when I say,
In spite of high station,
Rank and education,
She always spelt Cunt with a K.

There was a lady from Nagpur,
Who got laid by an alligator.
But nobody knew,
The result of that screw,
Because after sex, he ate her.

There once was a man from Bombay,
Who fashioned a cunt out of clay.
But the heat of his prick,
Turned it into a brick,
And it chafed his foreskin away.

There was a young woman named Sapphire,
Who succumbed to her lover's desire.
She said, "It's a sin,
But now that it's in,
Could you go a few inches higher?"

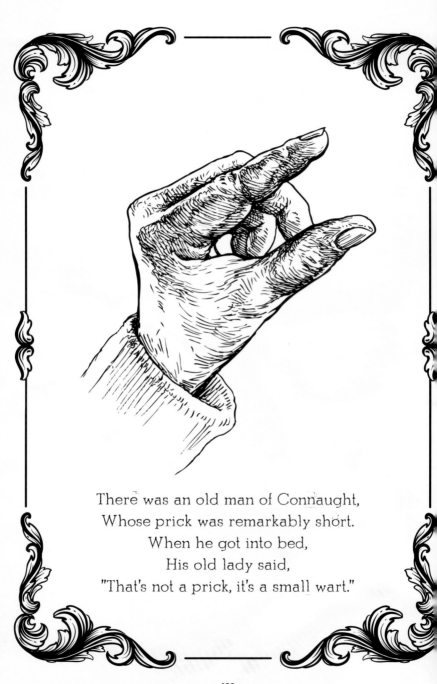

There was an old man of Connaught,
Whose prick was remarkably short.
When he got into bed,
His old lady said,
"That's not a prick, it's a small wart."

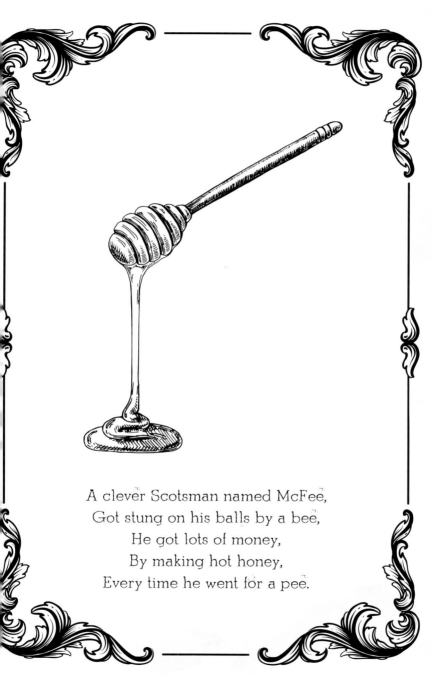

A clever Scotsman named McFee,
Got stung on his balls by a bee,
He got lots of money,
By making hot honey,
Every time he went for a pee.

There was an endowed man from Kent,
Whose cock was so long that it bent,
To save the girl trouble,
He put it in double
And instead of coming, he went!

There was a young man from the Clyde,
Who fell in a sewer and died.
The next day his brother,
Fell into another,
And now they're lying side by side.

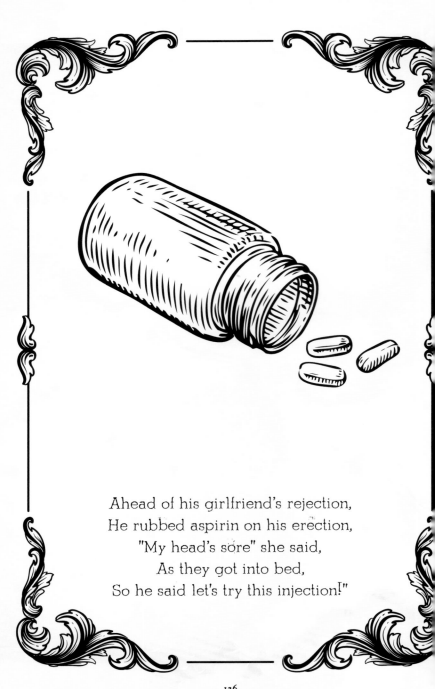

Ahead of his girlfriend's rejection,
He rubbed aspirin on his erection,
"My head's sore" she said,
As they got into bed,
So he said let's try this injection!"

There was a young woman of Thrace,
Who's corset was too tight to lace.
Her mother said "Nellie,
There's more in your belly,
Than ever went in through your face".

An eager young fella named Wayne,
Each day sought a girl to inflame!
All his dreams turned to ash,
They were gone in a flash!
'Cause his doll was filled with with propane!

There once was a girl named Twiggy,
Who liked to get down and jiggy.
She had sex with a hog,
And was blessed with a sprog,
Who was born half stick, half piggy!

There once was a man called Sonny,
Whose spunk was rather quite runny.
His wife shouted "Fuck it,
Just get me a bucket,
Let's sell it to earn some money"!

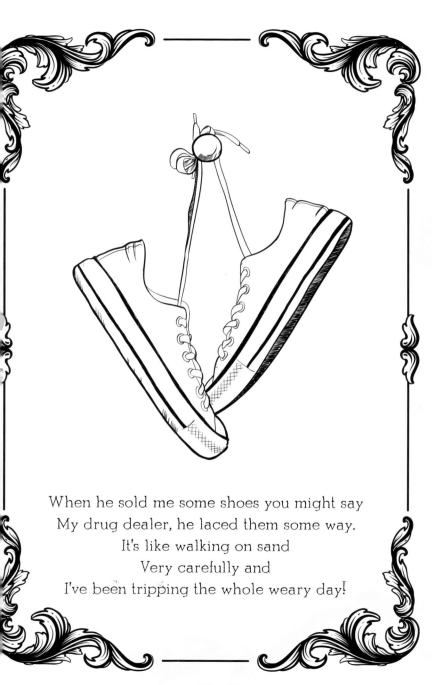

When he sold me some shoes you might say
My drug dealer, he laced them some way.
It's like walking on sand
Very carefully and
I've been tripping the whole weary day!

There once was a man from Calcutta
Who was caught jerking in a gutter.
The tropical heat,
Affected his meat,
So instead of cream he got butter!

There once was a hungry man named Keith,
Who gave circumcisions with his teeth.
It wasn't for leisure,
Or sexual pleasure,
But to get to the cheese underneath.

There once was a farmer named Lucket,
Saw a pig and wanted to fuck it.
The pig said "I'm queer,
But not from the rear,
Come round to the front and I'll suck it."

There once was a bishop from Kings,
Who talked about god and such things,
But his real desire,
Was a boy in the choir,
With a bum like jello on springs.

There was this baker from South Carolina,
Who stuck an eggbeater in her vagina.
The muffins she would glaze,
In an orgasmic haze,
And her screams, they would rattle the china!

One day I was feeling quite randy,
I went to the place I had handy.
Not a well thought out plan,
Just a windowless van,
That said "come in 4 some free candy."

There was a young lady of Harrow.
Who moaned that her cunt was too narrow,
For times without number,
She'd use a cucumber,
But could not accomplish a marrow.

There was a strong man of Drumrig,
Who one day did seven times frig;
He buggered three Sailors,
A nun and two Tailors,
And ended by fucking a pig.

There was a young man from Cape Horn
Who wished he had never been born.
And he would not have been
If his father had seen
That the end of the rubber was torn.

There was an old woman from Ealing
Who had a peculiar feeling
She sat on a chair,
Her legs in the air,
And pissed up all over the ceiling

There was a young maid of Shallott
Who lived upon shit, piss, and snot.
When these failed to please,
She'd lick the green cheese
She'd scraped with a spoon from her twat.

The was an old whore from Azóres
Whose cunt was all covered in sóres.
The cats of the street
Won't eat the green meat
That hung in festoóns from her drawers.

These limericks might be lewd,
But don't be misconstrued.
I bid you farewell,
I'll see you in hell,
Away from all the prudes!